On M. G. Stephens

Circles End, prose

"That opening in the oyster bar has whetted expectations."
  SEAMUS HEANEY

Jigs & Reels, short lyrical prose

"What instantly catches and pleases me is the detail, the way it is all specific, like they say, and is equally that lovely feel of *let me tell you...*"
  ROBERT CREELEY

After Asia, poetry (1993)

"The collection proceeds at a leisurely pace, enchanting and wholly believable."
  PUBLISHERS WEEKLY

"...wonderful...I very much enjoyed the poems."
  ANNIE DILLARD

Shipping Out, novel

"*Shipping Out* is beautiful. A gem. I love this book. It has the elegance and strength of the sea."
  Hubert Selby Jr.

"*Shipping Out* calls for reading and re-reading. Its density is such that images emerge on a second or third reading that are missed in the first. It has a richness and complexity to rival most recent poetry, let alone prose."
  Luc Sante, American Book Review

"Stephens has a prose imagination second to none. You've never read a sea story like this one; what's more, it's obviously more truth than fiction, which makes it doubly disturbing."
  Seymour Krim

Still Life, novel

"*Still Life* is a painfully comic gem of a novel."
 Walter Abish

Season at Coole, novel

"Lesser novelists faced with this array of characters would be content with merely depicting the decay of familial relationships. Mr. Stephens weaves them into a poem that soars. Out of remarkable bits and pieces—the interior monologues, the vivid scatological imagery, the impressionistic dialogue—there emerges a Coole *gestalt* that is far more than the sum of its sad ingredients."
 NEW YORK TIMES SUNDAY BOOK REVIEW

"It's an eloquent style that calls for reading aloud, an urban Irish style perhaps, perfect for nipping out the back door, rolling garbage cans as obstacles after you, and loping over the rooftops to safety in a vacant lot."
 ROLLING STONE

"Don't touch this book unless you value genuine talent wherever it shows. But it can't be denied. It shows."
 L. A. TIMES

"A host of colorful, depressing, funny, but always original characters."
 PUBLISHERS WEEKLY

"This first novel, scarcely promoted on publication, is a modern comic masterpiece of Irish family life."
 RICHARD ELMAN, *Gentleman's Quarterly*

"...a magniloquent, malignant rant, somewhere between James Joyce expatiated and Richard Pryor on a roll."
 NEWSDAY

"A bravura novel, funny and wild and language is its pole star, language that careens with a mad, sweet Irish lilt."
 KIRKUS REVIEWS

"A very beautiful novel, heartbreaking and comic, which is no easy thing to do."
GILBERT SORRENTINO

"Fantastic, astonishing, powerful...shines with honesty, craft, talent and love."
JOEL OPPENHEIMER

The Brooklyn Book of the Dead, novel

"It is a joy to read because Michael Stephens is such a superb writer, a master of language, in short, a poet. In his immaculate artistry he has given us another way of perceiving our lives and our struggle, forcing us to ask ourselves what our legacy will be."
HUBERT SELBY JR., author of Last Exit to Brooklyn

"The Brooklyn Book of the Dead is a cruelly funny, wrenchingly sad, yet beautiful work of fiction."
GILBERT SORRENTINO, author of Mulligan Stew

"Michael Stephens was my Dante into dark and dangerous places that native Irish writers never knew."
FRANK MCCOURT, author of Angela's Ashes

"This beautiful, cruel book—classical in form, Celtic in language, Brooklyn-American in content—is Michael Stephens's best book and may well be a masterpiece. It's like a pit bull on a chain, and you can lose a hand if you try to pet it. Read it carefully, warily."
RUSSELL BANKS, author of Affliction and Continental Drift

Lost in Seoul and Other Discoveries on the Korean Peninsula, travel memoir

"Michael Stephens teaches us how to look at things we have never seen before—and to make them part of what we know about ourselves."
PAUL AUSTER, author of The New York Trilogy

"*Lost in Seoul* is *terrific*—alive, great details, poignant..."
    ANNE WALDMAN

"Mr. Stephens himself is a bard, and this is a poet's evocation of Korea: personal, profound and—not to be forgotten—very funny."
    NEW YORK TIMES SUNDAY BOOK REVIEW

"In this exceptionally winning book, novelist Michael Stephens (*Season at Coole*) accompanies his Korean-born wife back to Seoul to meet her extended family. The result is a non-academic, thoroughly personal, rather winsome portrait of a Korean clan and of the society in which they live. Even readers with little interest in Korea will find Stephens's book both delightful and memorable."
    WASHINGTON POST BOOK WORLD

"A wonderful fusion of observation and poetry. Nothing I've read about Korea comes close to the pleasures and insights—the pleasures of insight—Stephens's book affords."
    RICHARD GILMAN, critic and Yale professor

"Stephens has his own American voice in which he delivers bright, compassionate, and often very funny cross-cultural history."
    MAUREEN HOWARD, novelist and essayist

Where the Sky Ends, memoir

"A brilliant, scorching, tremendously funny and moving story of alcoholism as a family disease told by a superbly gifted writer and survivor."
    ANN DOUGLAS, author of *Terrible Honesty: Mongrel Manhattan in the 1920s*

"Stephens's unrelenting analysis of what went wrong in a family nearly wrecked by alcohol made me realize that the possibility of change requires staring into the dark places not only without self-deception but with a willingness to forgive. This is a ferocious story gracefully told."
    STEPHEN DOBYNS, poet and novelist, author of *Velocities* and *The Church of Dead Girls*

"Michael Stephens is one of the most consistently powerful and self-insightful personal essayists in America. This memoir is as essential as it is unnerving, as generous as it is astringent."
 PHILLIP LOPATE, author of *The Art of the Personal Essay*

"In *Where the Sky Ends*, Michael Stephens—poet, novelist, playwright—has brought the force of all his talent to rendering this harsh yet regenerative family story with generosity and hard-won wisdom."
 MAUREEN HOWARD, author of *Facts of Life*

"To those who know Michael Stephens's work, it will come as no surprise that he has written, with his usual brave honesty, the story that our literature has been circling around for some time now. *Where the Sky Ends* is Stephens's *Long Night's Journey into Day*, a restorative narrative that looks the demon of family alcoholism square in the eye and stares it down with a ferocious clarity and compassion."
 RICHARD HOFFMAN, author of *Half the House: A Memoir*

The Dramaturgy of Style: Voice in Short Fiction, essays

"I wish Michael Stephens would stop re-routing subway lines inside the city of literature and giving the rest of us head-down trudgers terminal dread. We have our safe stereotypes to cling to, why can't he let us alone? Here he's gone and upset the purity of those venerable destinations—poetry, drama, fiction—with some subversive notion of literary miscegenation. The brass of this disrespectful Irishman is a thing to wonder at and warn against."
 SEYMOUR KRIM

"I suspect it is a work of absolute genius. Everything flows in exactly the right way; i.e., the content, form(s), language, images, tone, sound, the whole thing."
 HUBERT SELBY JR.

TOP BOY

M. G. Stephens

SPUYTEN DUYVIL
New York City

ACKNOWLEDGEMENTS

Some of these poems have appeared in the following magazines, for which the author wishes to thank their editors:

Ducts
Exquisite Corpse
Gargoyle
Subterranean Blue Poetry
Talisman
Hanging Loose
Notre Dame Review
Assisi
Insolent Aardvark
New York Writers Workshop
The Deadly Writers Patrol
Uncensored Song
Cicatrix
Hinchas de poesia
Kinship of Rivers
DeCasp

©2017 M.G. Stephens
ISBN 978-1-944682-71-2

Library of Congress Cataloging-in-Publication Data

Names: Stephens, Michael Gregory, author.
Title: Top boy / M. G. Stephens.
Description: New York City : Spuyten Duyvil, [2017]
Identifiers: LCCN 2017025932 | ISBN 9781944682712
Classification: LCC PS3569.T3855 A6 2017 | DDC 811/.54--dc23
LC record available at https://lccn.loc.gov/2017025932

Top Boy

Contents

Poetry	1
Expanding Outward	2
O Goddess Guide Me Home	3
Still Life with Pears	4
Fox in Garden	5
Soba Noodles	6
Top Boy	7
Chuang Tzu's Way	8
Your Smile Is a Papyrus	9
A Man Walks into a Bar	10
Sentimental Landscape in Brown	11
Flatlands Avenue	12
Peeling the Onion	13
Tornado Alley	14
April Thoughts in Moonlight Reflecting in a Pond	15
The Glass Ceiling	16
Hearing Voices Seeing Things	17
Whistler's Brother	18
When You Are Tired of London	19
In the Middle of My Life	20
Seaview	21
The Lazzo of the Weeping Crack Addict	22
Sand Dunes / Beach Grass	23
Oh What a Night	24
The Half-Full Life	25
The Ratman of Camden	26
The State of the Union	27
Tragedy	28
Like as the Moon	29
Dance with a Stranger	30
Rosita de Broadway	31

Breathing, Moving, Bursting	32
Westwind	33
A Letter to the Muse	34
Check It Out	35
All the Hooligans	36
Emperor Yao and My Grandfather	37
Street-Corner Aria	38
August 2014	39
A Wheeze from the Camden Geezer	40
Sitting across from the Muse, a Jay Flew into the Room	41
The Sycamore Tree	42
Why	43
The Nudes	44
The Hummingbird	45
Divorce	46
Day Moved into Evening	47
The Blue Rigi	48
Bird in Bird Bath	49
Losses	50
Endless Universe	51
A Portrait of the Muse	52
Paradiso	53
A Blue Expanse of Sky	54
Kilburn in the Summer	55
The New Moon	56
Woonsocket Moon Sonnet	57
The Muse's Eye	58
Dog Bone Sonnet	59
Moonholes at Morning Light	60
The Angles of the Moon	61
Life Sentence	63
Musings	64
The Moon on the Water	65

Golden State	66
Rat's Nest	67
The Fecking Rain	68
The Paradigm of the Raincoat	69
The Rumble	70
Molesworth Street Jump	71
Lazarus	72
I Told You So	73
The River	74
Morning Light Through Saloon Windows	75
What I Miss	76
The Scarlet Tanager	77
Six Million	78
Herons and Gladiolas	79
Lunch	80
The Tao of the Taoiseach	81
There Is No Muse Like This Muse	82
Sailing to Brooklyn	83
The Migration of Birds	84
Finn McCoole	85
Danny Boy	86
Pre-Owned	87
What Is Light	88
After a Merce Cunningham Concert in London	89
Pearly Luster	90
The Jumpshooter's Nightmare	91
Susan's Sonnet	92
A Bad Case of the Blues	93
What Is Possible	94
The Lark	95
Just Now But Not Always	96
A Pig on the Sofa	97
Gravity	98

The Empty Room	99
Shooting Star in the Blue Night's Sky	100
Your Mouth Is a Wave	101
Urbane	102
The Muse as Castalian Spring	103

Poetry

I no longer believe in anything
But you, and you are shape-shifting away
In a dazzling corner of the room,
Which otherwise is quite empty of life.

You strip from your clothes and stand there almost
Naked but for polka-dotted knickers,
Inviting me to fall in love with you
Just one last time, please, all over again.

I have been around the world many times,
Been shot at in demilitarized zones,
Boogie-boarded my way through green-blue surf,
And sat alone in gray one-lightbulb rooms,

All to show my adoration of you,
And here I am once more at your altar.

Expanding Outward

The heart has nothing to do with it as
It goes on pumping whether you are here
Or not, but the head hurts and the stomach
Turns over upon itself and time heals
Nothing, being neutral, and space around
Things becomes greater, expanding outward,
While the moon rises and sets, the stars come
And go as they please, and the spring follows
The last gasps of winter just as summer
Comes and goes, dropping down into autumn,
Winter once more upon us, the heart still
Pumping and having nothing to do with
Love or you or anything that once seemed
To matter so much and doesn't at all.

O Goddess Guide Me Home

Often I think of the Muse, her pale flesh,
Her blue-green-blue-gray eyes, hair billowing
Out in this sort of reverie, as one
Might imagine, there is no avoiding
Such billowing hair in this kind of love

Poem, much as I might wish to give her
Another style of haircut or turn her
Eyes a different color or make the
Hair less billowy, it streams out behind
Her like an angel's wing, and when the moon

Appears, the blue stars come out in the night
Sky, exploding like firecrackers up there,
While down below, I am sat thinking of
The Muse, O goddess, guide me home to peace
And serenity, bring me an ounce of

Sobriety in that frothy gold cup,
Let me lick the salt off your ruby lips.

Still Life With Pears

The pears hang from the tree in the garden
in the leaden summer air, waiting to
drop onto the wet August grass; a fox
lingers by the fence watching the fat pears

like it was a physicist, pondering
Newton's laws, Einstein's relativity,
and maybe even a little chaos
theory, too, studying the garden fruits

as if they were asteroids or planets,
not fat summer pears bursting their covers,
but fat waiters bursting from tight jackets

or plump teenagers bursting white dresses
moments before their dates arrive, surly
and drunk, demanding favors and sodas.

Fox In Garden

Each morning outside our back window, a fox
and her cub appear in the little garden on
the edge of the Hampstead Heath, sunning there

until a noise or movement frightens them
away into the underbrush until
the next time when they appear once again.

We had been living down the road from here
in a smaller flat, landlady horrible,
no space to breathe, so this was a godsend.

How odd to think that our landlady's name
was also Fox, dragging about her cub,
a little five-year-old boy, her one bit

of saving grace and humanity.
All the rest of her was mean and greedy.

Soba Noodles

I was to meet Richard at the Chinese
restaurant on Mass Ave off Harvard Square,
and I'd just come from the noon meeting at
the Lutheran church. This was not Eliot's

midwinter thaw, but a ravaging winter
day in January, wet, raw, and cold.
Snow mounds piled sky high, I heard a peep, then
an incredible silence, its wing passed

over me, and I looked out of the edge
of my vision, and I saw a raptor,
small but tough, snatch a sparrow in its claws,

talons like hooks, and then glide through backyards
and behind apartment houses, flying
away to eat. I was hungry now, too.

Top Boy

> "Practically every boy in the United States
> dreams of becoming our President."
> *Twelves Steps and Twelve Traditions*

In the second grade at St. Aidan's School,
I was picked as the top academic
Student to greet the President of the
United States as his motorcade drove

Past our grammar school on Long Island in
The early 1950s. President
Dwight Eisenhower, along with his wife
Mamie, drove up Willis Avenue in

A Cadillac convertible. He asked
Me what I wanted to be when I grew
Up, and I said, "A tramp." There was a long

Pause before a Sister of Charity
Shewed me away from the car, Ike and his
Entourage speeding off for the North Shore.

Chuang Tzu's Way

Yes, there were nine children I grew up with,
but years later I asked my mother how

many children she had, including those
who died in infancy or right out of

the womb, and she paused before answering,
then mom asked her literary son,

"Are you writing another book about
us?" and I said, no, but I was lying,

and so she told me then, "Sixteen in all."
Back when there were only seven of us,

we had to share one giant-sized bed, and
so my father let us sleep in shifts of

three at a time in the bed, and later
the last four got their turn. But they balked.[1]

---

[1] So my father, usually a man who had no sense of compromise, even though he had gone to Georgetown for a year to study to be a diplomat, came up with a novel idea of letting the four sleep first, and the other three children last. The four complainers, though still four to the bed, never complained again, and the three others waited, if not patiently, they waited and waited, until it was their turn to sleep, sometimes falling off asleep standing up, homework falling all about the bare wood floors of our little old house, and no one stirred, except a fat old mouse.

Your Smile Is A Papyrus

My fingers tell a story as they walk
Across the desert between your stomach
And your neck, but then reach an oasis
Of your breasts, and the palm trees of your eyes,

The figs your ears are, the dates of your lips.
Your smile is a papyrus uncovered,
And your legs are an isthmus of ideas,
Challenging imagination's own fears.

My tongue goes on another kind of trip
Across these personal Saharas, salt
And sand, wind and dust blowing through your hair,

I lick your thighs and taste your eyes, the moon
Rising across the night sky as we dance
In place, dreaming of oceans far away.

A Man Walks Into A Bar

A man walks into a bar and orders a shot of whiskey
With a beer chaser bartender sets him up

Man drinks whiskey drinks beer passes out with his head resting
On the bar you can't do that says the bartender

Shaking the man awake in that case the man says
Just give me a haircut and forget about the shave

Sentimental Landscape In Brown

Landscape burnt umber and amber and brown,
winter in the air, but no snow on ground
yet. Sky pearly. November in New York.
Destitutes cold and edgy, hungry and

lonely. Lose your mind on the crystal train.
Light a candle in the skull. Remind you
of Norman Rockwell, does it? Kind of feel
like a Hallmark greeting card, the hollow

eyes of the poor following your coattails?
If only Charlie Chaplin were here to
render it into cinematic art.

Umber and amber and somber and brown.
Maybe Walt Disney has some mistletoe.
Even the white people look miserable.

Flatlands Avenue

Head in the toilet at my Uncle Tom's
house in Flatbush after his oldest child
Regina, nicknamed Jeannie, was married
at the Knights of Columbus hall, Flatlands
Avenue, two blocks away, I puked and puked
my guts out as a Franciscan priest named
Father Lucian—my Uncle Andy really—
lectured me on the sin of gluttony.

Yet how could you drink too much alcohol?
Was that possible? There never was enough
as far as I was concerned, even at
that age, I had to have a lot to fill
the hole in my soul, bigger than legends
like Sugar Ray Robinson or Gil Hodges.

Peeling The Onion

If you peel away layers of onion,
you will come to its core, and once that is
done, there is nothing, not even essence
of what once was the onion. Peer Gynt led

such a life. He peeled away the layers of his
existence, hoping to discover his
essence, but he found nothing, or worse than
nothingness, he found the empty center

of the human dilemma, a moment
that was filled with terror, not unlike the
old Jews, some of whom, it was claimed, stared
at the face of God, and were horrified.

Whom did they expect, Alec Baldwin?
Was it written God had to be handsome?

Tornado Alley

When you are going it alone
through a great whirlwind,

There is nothing like a poem
to focus the mind.

April Thoughts In Moonlight Reflecting In A Pond

1.
It may well be however I get there,
Khakis and my blue heaven, whenever
Bars and the moon up above, my blue shirt,
Chuckles, M & M's, Good & Plenty, Mars,

Dungarees and Keds sneakers, Snickers and
Cruel as blue suede shoes and twice as cool as
And green stems and lovely, they are also
The tulips are blue and red and purple.

2.
The tulips are blue and red and purple
And green stems and lovely, they are also
Cruel as blue suede shoes and twice as cool as
Dungarees and Keds sneakers, Snickers and

Chuckles, M & M's, Good & Plenty, Mars
Bars and the moon up above, my blue shirt,
Khakis and my blue heaven, whenever
It may well be however I get there.

The Glass Ceiling

"I went up the long wooden stairwell to the top floor of the dormitory
where I hoped to look at the winter sky,

the heavens, and many stars on this clear night, but when I got up to the top floor
        the door was locked, and instead of stars and

the vault of heaven, I saw the ceiling, the glass ceiling that allowed me to
        go no further than I had come until

now. I am lost about what to do in the land of the slam-dunk and McDonald's,
        Kentucky Fried chicken and burritos,

go home or stay, knowing that where I have come to is as far as I am to go."

Hearing Voices Seeing Things

I raised my hand and was called on, and so
I asked the therapist this question
from my seat in the back of the gray room:
if prayer is speaking to God, and we say
that meditation is listening to
Him, I wanted to know what they called it
if this Higher Power—oh Great Spirit!—
spoke back to us. What was that response called?

(I thought of statues in a Franciscan
monastery on the Hudson River
where I had gone for a spiritual
retreat, and how I was so anxious
I thought they might speak to me then and there.)

A patient called out: "Schizophrenia!"

Whistler's Brother

I was out walking on Sunday morning
when I heard someone whistling,
           not just whistling, but doing it beautifully,

and when I turned to look who was doing it,
I saw an old white-haired man on a tandem
           bicycle, first with an older woman

who wore a bonnet, and later along Broadway,
him alone, whistling, not like a maniac,
           but like a consummate musician, really

the most beautiful whistling I ever heard,
and him slowly moving up Broadway
           on his tandem bicycle, only now alone,

whistling and moving slowly along,
I saw and heard and felt him as I walked.

When You Are Tired Of London

When you are tired of London,
there is no need to go to Eastbourne
(Susan was stung by a wasp there).

You pack up your books, clothes,
manuscripts, and household effects.
You put everything into a half container

that will be shipped across the bitter sea
for New York or Cleveland. There is no long
goodbye, not even a farewell handshake.

When you are tired of London,
you are not tired of life, but you maybe need
Paris, pine for New York, shuffle off

not to Buffalo, but Chicago (well, Evanston,
just to its north). There remain residues
of gratitude, calm and serenity, but also

this uncontrollable anger about what might have
been, though never was. You fume and steam
and stamp long enough, then you go without

pomp, without a thought of ever returning,
the romance ended, the engagement off,
when you are tired of London.

In The Middle Of My Life

The Muse and I dine al fresco, Perrin's
Walk, Hampstead, and I feed her carrot cake,
Pots of Earl Grey (milk on the side), humus

And pita bread, and we talk and laugh and
Wile away the afternoon and our lives,
As if we didn't have a care in the world,

Which in a sense is true, as it is in
The middle of the week, in the middle
Of the day at a still point in our lives,

So we are sat there eating and talking,
Drinking buckets of tea, the Muse herself
Beautiful and unobtainable, blue

Footed and sure of herself, cool and, like
Maud Gonne, she is there and not there and gone.

Seaview

Yo, girlfriend,
Who/s yr
gull friends?

The Lazzo Of The Weeping Crack Addict

How cruel we have become in this season! I walk past the weeping man on the corner as if he were a gargoyle on the side of a building. Yet I have passed him too many times this winter, and he's always weeping like that, deeply and sickly pathetic, his voice lunging at you as you pass, begging and weeping, please, please, please, he says, just a morsel, just a crumb, just a penny, I'm starving, I have no food, not eaten in days, I have not slept in a bed in weeks, I have fallen on bad times. I stumbled, just like Jesus on the road to Calvary. I'll get back on my feet.

Sand Dunes / Beach Grass

Boston's gray day broke with a radiance
that did not come from sky but from this face
by the doorway of the office, telling
about her summer near Blackfish Creek, and

it made one think of how the pilot whales
beached themselves every January
near this part of Cape Cod Bay. But it was
not simply the beached whales that came washing

back over me; I also thought of my
old friend Deborah whom I've not seen for
two decades, and her family's houses

at the shore, on the dune, nothing but sky
and sea, sand and Shore Road, and the other
house in town next door to the Wilsons' house.

Oh What A Night

No one falls in love anymore because
It is such a ridiculous notion
So imagine his surprise when this bird
Taps him on the shoulder and asks to dance
Sure he said not knowing his left foot from
His right or what the proper figures were
For instance the box step or the cha-cha
So again imagine his surprise when
At the end of the dance he already
Was halfway towards being in love with
This bird and by the end of evening
They were inseparable soulmates two
Peas in a pod the yin to that one's yang
And they barely knew each other's first names

The Half-Full Life

1.
Take the melancholic type, despairing, full of ennui, tristeste, and the ache so full it is like a rheum. Or like a dark, gloomy room, full of old hurts and pains from past resentments never healed. It all comes down to what Ernest Hemingway once said: It is good. It is very good. It was once good, that is. Now it is not good at all. It is bad. Very bad. Is that when he pulled the trigger? Or did he say that day that the Idaho sky was overcast and I think I'll die. Yet it is good; it is very good; it is very very good, indeed, that is, until it gets bad.

2.
What I have left then is a life, not a half-life even if more than half my life has been spent and even wasted, though each breath I take is precipitated on inalienable assumptions that everything from here out is a gift and nothing more nor less, simply a tiny miracle grown vast in my eyes and head and even some days in my heart, so that the light I crave is inward, air I breathe is outside, the friends I make are free of the old plague of booze stalking us like a cloaked and hooded assassin. The romance is not about booze but you.

Ratman Of Camden

Susan first heard something in the kitchen
under the sink, like a drunken father
stumbling about, only in camera,
under wraps. Afterward, I had to look
for evidence and I found it, rat shit
and rags soiled by their visit to our flat.

Months went by, and I saw no sign of them.
Then I opened a drawer, and it was filled
with their droppings, so I called the Council,
and they sent Ian the Ratman over
to address our pest problem, dropping bags
of blood coagulant, i.e., poison.

First they swarmed outside the bedroom window.
Then they got droopy and went really slow.

The State Of The Union

Clockwise, the ambassador stands next to
The spymaster's mistress, a double-agent
Provocateur, and behind the clot of
Gerberas and gentians, that gentle

Man is the spymaster himself, a tall
Fellow with willowy build, gargantuan
Gait, pinstriped and bow-tied, like a present,
Be-ringed and with an expensive gold watch,

A Swiss one with multiple functions, very
James Bond. All of these pillars of social
And civic probity are involved up

To their eyeballs and ears in unseemly
Things like death squads, torture by waterboard
And extreme rendition, here and abroad.

Tragedy

Knock-knock.
Who's there?
Hamlet.
Hamlet *who*?
Your dead father.

Like As The Moon

1.
My whole attitude drifts into a new lunar phase, benign to all concerned.

2.
True, I am a lunatic. But that's only half the story.

3.
I have brown eyes, what does that tell you about me?

4.
Nothing, I say.

5.
All it informs you about is that my eyes are not blue.

6.
The moon rises; it's full, and it drifts over the landscape as I drift toward conflict, losing all hope, then sets.

7.
Hopelessly unresolved, but like the moon, our moods change with our skyward positions, life changes with new seasons, waxing and waning, i.e., we're alive, the moon and me, and I carry myself differently.

Dance With A Stranger

A week or two later I stood in front
of the Magdala, placing my finger
into the crevices of two bullet
holes I forgot to show my New York friends.

The bullets were chambered by Ruth Ellis,
the last woman in England to be hanged,
the other bullets having penetrated
her lover's heart as she executed

him for his human transgressions, wander-
lust turned lethal. Remember that movie
Dance with a Stranger, and the empty world

Miranda Richardson portrayed so well?
It is raining again in North London,
and outside it is very cold tonight.

Rosita De Broadway

And the sun out, sky blue like it hasn't been for weeks, and the temperature is threatening the seventies for the first time this year, though it's always springtime on the Number Five bus, and it's always sunny outside, it seems, even when it rains in other places in the city.

I get off the bus in Morningside Heights, and walk to Broadway and my apartment a few blocks away on Cathedral Parkway. I stop into Rosita de Broadway and order a cafe con leche, while the waitress Carmen tells me about her own life of joy and sadness and fever.

Breathing, Moving, Bursting

This one is different from the others,
for they are dead; she is alive and well.
Her stride is different than their strides were;

she is more lunar or more like flowers
that seek the light, shifting to absorb heat
into their core, breathing, moving, sometimes

bursting into a song or tears or anger
like that of a mangy old dog, all smell
and tongue-crazed, a terrible muttish cur.

She is crazy but full of edges like a knife,
and her teeth gleam like stars or the new moon.
Oh, she is different all right; mothers

run indoors when they see her on the prowl,
stretching toward the moon like midnight's hours.

Westwind

Along / among
Below the sky

The clouds about
Wind pulls me

And birds in flight

A Letter To The Muse

I had wanted to write to let you know
That all is well, despite adversity
Of one sort or another, and I write
Because you are on my mind once again,
And as is often the case these days, hours
Go by in this way, and even days pass
Without a thought for anything much else
But this, until I snap back to the world.

I am about to leave on a long trip
Momentarily and will be away
For a time, and since you are my big-footed
Muse, I want to let you know how much
I appreciate your company and
Inspiration over cups of Earl Grey.

Check It Out

Check out the gladiolas, day lilies
and daffodils mixed with the smell of meat
and the greengrocer's pushcarts, running shoes
and nylon sports gear that fell off the back
of a slow lorry the night before last
and wound up fifty percent off list price
from the high street.
Hey, check it out, slip-ons
for a fraction of the higher asking
price and Ben Sherman shirts that look as good
as the real thing.
    Hey, my friend, check it out.

Plastic gangsters meet plastic paddies, meet
Al Qaida and Irish grandmas, market
capitalists speculating on flats
at the open-air market.
    Check it out.

All The Hooligans

All the babies my mother had (fifteen of them born in St. Mary's Bed-Stuy, so many they should have named a ward for my mother, though I—being more perverse than even the relatives' forgotten language—was born in Washington, D.C. after World War II, the only one of her sixteen children to dream up such a wacky idea) and all the hooligans my red-haired crazy-hearted aunts indulged and entertained in their own mother's place and my Gaeltacht grandmother cursing life, the world, and everyone, first English cursed, then Yiddish, finally in Irish.

Emperor Yao And My Grandfather [2]

    Wise Yao ruled China, wide and far, taming
the world into a kind of natural
peace and order. Afterward, he trotted

    off to visit the four perfections in
a far-away mountain range of Ku Shih.
When Yao returned from his journey, crossing

    the borderline back into his city,
his empty gaze dwelt upon this simple
and odd fact: There was no more throne!

    Nothing remained of the world that he had
once known so well. In this sense, he reminds
me of grandfather who went out one day,

    only to be so utterly transformed
by what he once thought the quotidian.

---

[2] *Fin-de-siècle* New Yorker, bailbondsman, realtor, a haberdasher, my grandfather came upon a line of top-grade hats of felt construction, loden-green and navy-blue and mouse-gray hats from Europe or of the European styles: fedoras and borsalinos, etc. Grandfather grabbed a pile of hats and went to South Brooklyn, visiting a gang of crazy men with shaved heads and naked girls, ship anchors, and hearts tattooed on their arms, arrows piercing these hearts, legends telling of Mom, Angela, Deirdre, or Mary. What did these men care about the hatter?

Street-Corner Aria

He is like Harlequin, only better, and he is like the Cooks and
Servants, a kind of poor man's Pagliacci, he sings for a bit of rock,
though instead of tears that cry out, Figaro! Figaro! he sings
for crack, some crystals in a plastic vial with a colorful top, the street
littered with the vials, and he becomes, once again, strung out,
and he goes back to Broadway to weep and cry. He calls out: "Help
me, help me, don't walk by and ignore me! Where is your sense of
humanity? I am a human being. I am not a dog or a rat. I'm like you,
only for me it's bad times."

August 2014

August the second
Twenty-fourteen four p.m.—
A myrtle warbler

A Wheeze From The Camden Geezer

If he howled at the moon,
Could he be any madder
Than he is, with a crazy tune
Going through his head like a shredder.

Here he stands in his old socks,
A man who has reached three and a half
Score years, his head full of sex,
And his belly twisted by love's shaft.

You see the young making plans
In the cafes of their desires, kissing
On the sofas on Parkway in Camden,
And outside rain spits, wind hissing.

The moment he leaves the café,
Everyone breaks into collective
Laughter, calling him daffy,
Or worse yet, restorative.

Sitting Across From The Muse, A Jay Flew Into My Room

The jay sat on the door handle inside
The room, cackling softly as it took
In this surprising human nest,
Its body a tawny color with bright

Colorful wing feathers. The supermoon
Had not yet risen up into the sky,
And my heart was like a stone as I held
My breath and did not move, trying to see

Your lips which was what I was thinking of
When the jay first appeared by the brown door
That led onto a quite small balcony.

I had imagined trying to draw you
When suddenly the jay landed on the
Handle, and it was as if time stood still.

The Sycamore Tree

The crow was killed and eaten by falcons,
And a falcon was killed and eaten by
A bunch of crows, the only ones who know
The real story, and they aren't talking:

Other birds (starlings, cardinals, sparrows,
Etc.) have taken a vow of
Silence, making them seem almost like monks
Or mafia henchmen, they know nothing

About the stupid falcon, so children
And relatives of the raptor pick off
Crows like they were in a shooting gallery
At the penny arcade at the amusement

Park, or like drones in the sky out looking
For enemies of the homeland, so crows
Keep to themselves, their numbers dwindling
Day by day, sitting in the bare branches

Of the sycamore tree, silent as snow.

Why

We know how it happened, and where, over
there and down that long block a little ways,

and everyone knows it happened, there
is no argument about that, we know

who was there, what they said and did, and how
it all unfolded, moment to moment,

out back and around the corner and up
that grim dark alley where they congregate,

and when it all shook out, and the shit came
down, early afternoon into the next

evening, light turning from bright golden rays
into silvery illuminations,

almost a fog settled over all this
when we asked ourselves why them, why now, why?

The Nudes

They came down the staircase and were about
The studio, naked on couches, blue
Persian rugs, they sat on stools posing for
Artists and would-be artists alike, nudes
Walking on wooden floors or talking on
Their mobile telephones, men and women
Alike, standing in front of mirrors, two
And three of them at a time, laughing.

One of them reclines languidly over
There, leaning on the sofa's arm, smiling,
As another waves from a bike going
Nowhere (no wheels), only a frame, smoking
Cigarettes, drinking wine, laughing always
Laughing with *joie de vivre*, with real gusto.

The Hummingbird

In the gardens, as in love, the humming
Is below the human threshold, a blur
Then more than a hum, as a child races
From place to place, playing hide and seek, bird
Flits about, seeking the tree, the fountain,
As determined and as fast as our thoughts,
It moves about like the light, noiseless as
The sun, and as intense out of the shade,
It meditates on its own mayhem, blue
At one angle, iridescent yellow,
Red as sunset, the apple of the sky,
As in love with life as a child is in
Love with it, determined as an image
Of an after-image, a shadow or
A shade, a bolt of light, a blade, a hum.

Divorce

I lived with you because I couldn't live
Without you, but now I live without you
Because I can't live with you anymore.

A kestrel hovers outside my window,
And it follows me when I am outside,
I will have to chase it away one day.

Day Moved Into Evening

At the deep end of September, I found
Myself almost giddy with being here
And alive, just being in the after-
Glow of the late afternoon, moments from
October and further along the long slide to
Winter, which was anywhere but on my
Mind, this lighter than air occurrence in
The chill air and the still, gold sunlight.

I knew it would pass, but I couldn't believe
My luck as it lingered throughout the day,
Moment by moment unfolding out there
As the afternoon moved into evening,
And then it became night, and I hurried
To the window to see the supermoon.

The Blue Rigi

Writing like a painter, it's like dying
And going to heaven, at least poets
I know have said as much to me about
Such technique as that kind of light
Touch, Frank O'Hara comes almost to mind
Immediately, which is not the same
As painting as if one were a writer,
My idea of the blunt, heavy hand.

Turner painted in the plain air before
The majesty of Blue Rigi, water
And colour his media, making it
Look like it was oil paint, just as painting
In his hand was like bright watercolours,
Only taking forever to dry right.

Bird In Bird Bath

It was said that if I couldn't concentrate,
I should try to focus on one thing for
A minute, so I chose this young sparrow
That flitted from the water at my place
On to the balcony, up to the old Greeks
Balcony on the fifth floor, over to
The eaves above the pub on this estate,
Back to the old Greeks where it ate fat balls

Which he had put out next to bird feeder,
Then back to my balcony for water
To drink and later bathe in joyously,
So that the minute did not linger like
Others said it might but flew as fast as
The sparrow, and I was ready to work.

Losses

I seem to lose friends the way some people
Misplace a sock after doing laundry.

My old friends, my new friends, they disappear
The way you might lose a blue umbrella.

If the home team loses, I don't really
Care anymore who wins, I get on with

It, but this absence of the familiar
Seems to trouble my soul and my blank mind.

I seem to lose friends the way the others
Lose a lucky penny or a wish list.

My new friends, my old friends, they all seem to
Vanish like the stars in the sky when moon

Sets and the sun rises, and all go out
To work, while I sit here counting losses.

Endless Universe

As I awoke fully awake—rested,
There were stars in my eyes as a result
Of there still being no curtain on the
Window, so I got up and made some tea,
And as I sipped it, I turned off the light
In the kitchen and tip-toed across the
Linoleum floor to the small glass door
Onto the small balcony and the stars.

It had just then gone four in the morning,
And what was on offer at that moment
Was not the smallness, the pettiness, nor
The worthlessness of my short, humble life,
But instead the vastness of the night's sky,
And the endless universe out beyond.

A Portrait Of The Muse

If I remember correctly, the Muse
Has ginger-colored hair, the muscles of
A retired athlete, feet to conquer world
Problems with her creative solutions,

And hands as strong as undersea cables,
Eyes as piercing as arrows, though full of
Compassion and warmth, breasts as shapely as
Great works of art, which they certainly are.

But the artful, kind Muse has feet of clay,
And goes to the dentist regularly
For her check-up, a cavity here or

There, even the odd root canal once in
A blue moon, under which she stands calling
Out the poet—Oh, my god! Oh, MG!

Paradiso

Aged steaks live
Jazz old friends
All night long

A Blue Expanse Of Sky

There is no need to write or call me up
Because I won't answer or even be
There once more to receive your messages.

I'll be off on the Heath walking up hills
Or down them, staring at the clouds above,
Floating past in a blue expanse of sky

Or sitting on a bench looking to all
The world like a dotty old pensioner
Who hasn't had a reasonable thought

In donkey's years, and if I ever should
Happen to recall who you are, let it
Be with kindness and compassion, bitter

Recrimination not something I do
Well, though love is not my forte either.

Kilburn In The Summer

It was a hot, humid July, the air
So thick you could cut it as if it was
A loaf of bread or a telephone cord.

I was supposedly on vacation,
But took the train to work in order to
Interview for a higher position.

In the eyes of god we are all just one
People, neither higher nor lower than
Anyone else, but that's not how it worked

In this life, and that's not how the bombers
Saw it, blasting two trains and one bus; I
Was on the train going nowhere that day.

Back in Kilburn, an old Irish neighbor
Said, "They won't have us to blame for this one."

The New Moon

Tired of the old moon, here is a new one,
waxing and waning like the other moon,
yet somehow different than all the old
ones, this a blue-white laminate, a chill

with hope at its edges, even if it
appears to be darker and further from
you, a full moon colored by grief, carved out
of the imagination like paper

moons you hung from light fixtures when you were
a child, and the people you loved would live
forever, only to have you grow up

and find them gone, lost like an old blue coat
you once loved or else to have it stolen,
and you stand there, freezing and all alone.

Woonsocket Moon Sonnet

Hiya, Moon, I see you out the bedroom
Window, floating in the sky like candy
Made of white chocolate or I see you
In my other room and I think of skin
That I might lick, searching for your nipple.
But we are older now and should be more
Reserved, even though we are probably
Even less reserved than we ever were.

Sometimes I write poems about other
Things, but you know and I know that these are
Really poems about you, my true love,
And is why I painted a thousand portraits of
You up there, out there in the universe,
Cold and passionate, naked and alone.

The Muse's Eye

Lately I have advertised for a Muse,
And someone answered the ad, informing
Me that I was a sexist pig to be
Conducting business this way in the
21st century, and they had a
Point; I rewrote the ad accordingly:
Older male writer and collagist in
Market for a Muse, send me an email.

"Looking for a Muse, male, female or trans;
Age not important, though a sense of fun,
Intelligence and good taste are a must;
An ability to discern, if not
Right from wrong, then the good from the bad,
And, of course, an eye for the beautiful."

Dog Bone Sonnet

Sit.
Stay.
Shit.
Play.

Growl.
Bite.
Prowl.
Fight.

Eat.
Pee.
Sleep.
Flee.

Bark.
Park.

Moonholes At Morning Light

The woman associated with the
Moon is the purpose for whom this knowledge
Is relevant, to whom this note I write
Is written, about whom more anon: she
Swims naked in a lake in the moonlight.

She sings naked in the night below the
Moon, a kind of mermaid, a kind, gentle
Person, swimming across the lake at the
Speed of handwriting across a page; it's
For her lover. To her lover she sings.

Her lover is no man or woman, but
The moon itself for whom she swims naked
Across midnight's lake, a stroke here, a breath
There, almost as though she were dancing, not
Swimming alone amid moonlight out there.

The Angles Of The Moon

1. The Moon (Almost Full)

You lift up your arms towards the gibbous
Moon in the night sky a shape that is not
What it seems to be too full to be half
It is too shapeless to be really full

More like a wad of gum a blob of light
That is as uncertain as the weather
Misty and yet clear damp but dry the sky
A concatenation of white roses

And the moon it reaches out to you with
Its arm as milky as your own pale arm
Touching your gloved hand with its long white hand
Alive in the night with the electric

Purr of the planet spinning ever on
Towards the end of the day on our way
Home lounging towards our flat and its warmth
A cocoon of rooms to welcome us back

2. <u>Gibbous</u>

What it seems to be too full to be half
Alive in the night with the electric
More like a wad of gum a blob of light
Touching your gloved hand with its long fingers

That is as uncertain as the weather
You lift up your arms towards the gibbous
Moon in the night sky a shape that is not
A cocoon of rooms to welcome us back

Home lounging towards our flat and its warmth
Its arm as milky as your own pale arm
Misty and yet clear damp but dry the sky

Towards the end of the day on our way
Purr of the planet spinning ever on
It is too shapeless to be really full

Life Sentence

The supermoon came and went,
Now it's time to pay the piper,
That time of month to pay the rent,
Or to write before I run out of paper,
As I need something to show I'm a writer,

People, this is how my time is spent,
I worry about little things at all times
Of day and night, in every free moment,
Sometimes spending hours thinking of rhymes,
At other times, I do nothing, grunt

And am lazy as a criminal dreaming of crimes,
For instance, take this day, and how I bent
Time to conform to my schedule of dreams,
And how I sent shock waves through the tent
Of literature, confecting these hopeless schemes,

And it is not so much a crime against humanity,
As it is a shame I even wrote this piece of vanity.

Musings

There is no Muse like the old one, nothing
So reassuring as that familiar
Face, walking hand in hand down the local
Streets, our Rialto this avenue, our
Albion this city, our place in the
Universe right where we are located.

This is not to say that there are not things
Which need improving. I am a messy
Person, haphazard in my domestic
Circumstances, to say the least, I am
A work in progress, even as the good
Muse is a kind of human perfection.

But I make oatmeal in the morning, cook
Dinner, and try to be an open book.

The Moon On The Water

I am drunk, like Li Po, with the moon re-
Flected on the surface of the water
Along the lake, stone cold sober, yet drunk

On the Muse, dancing across my eyelids
Like a fucking Naiad, drunk on movement
Of the wind across the water, shitfaced

With the sound of the wind in the bare trees,
Intoxicated by lunar whispers
Across the softly breaking waves, the Muse

Beckoning across the water, "I am
The wind and the bare trees and the water,
And I am young and I am beautiful,

I am in love with you, oh, poet, write
Me a song, sing me a sonnet, carry
Me across the water on your lovely

Words tonight." So I wrote this poem, this
Song, but by the time I got back, she was
Gone, and so was the moon. So was the moon.

Golden State

The Oklahoma
Thunder have Curry's number—
Jumpshots do not drop

Rat's Nest

Everything is ace
It's where it hangs
Its hat its shitty hat

To the rat its nest
It's more than that
It's where it gnaws

The bone where it rests
Its weary ratty head
Where it lets go of day

The nest is not a mess
Not a hive of dysfunction
It's home sweet home

The Fecking Rain

It rains and rains quite a bit here, the rain
falls, cascades, plunges downward, down, down, down,
it rains and it rains and it rains some more,
it pours down or runs horizontally

from the fierce winds thrusting it along, winds
that are wet from the endless downpouring,
a deluge, really, plunging, cascading
as night falls and the rain keeps falling, too.

But let's not forget the writers either,
for when the rains come, they go off to write,
writing and writing, making this place as

famous for its writers as awful rain—
poets, fiction writers, essay writers,
and playwrights, writing in the fecking rain.

The Paradigm Of The Raincoat

I still find myself looking in windows
for that perfect raincoat, the paradigm,
the mother of all raincoats, not too long,
nor too short, green but not too green, khaki

would be fine with me or even loden,
yet saying that, I no longer care if
it's a Barbour or a London Fog, all
I care about is whether it keeps me

dry, looks passably good, say not too cheap,
so that I'd be turned away by doormen,
but not too fancy that muggers want it.

Salinger, in regard to the using
of his work without any permission:
it was like they stole his best overcoat.[3]

---

3   I have not spent my life searching for God, but I have spent half of it looking for a raincoat. Right now, I own at least three of them, all various shades of greeny construction, the Gore-Tex light green one from L.L. Bean, bought for a trip to Ireland one summer. Then there is the dark green one I got from Willis and Geiger, perfect, I once thought, until I noticed that it bunched and hung all wrong, a material that absorbed the cold as much as repelled the rain, which leaves the very last raincoat—it comes from Filson in Seattle, sent to replace one that wore out too early.

The Rumble

The red kite
Picked a fight

With a bull snake
What a big mistake!

Molesworth Street Jump

A game of Horse with Tony Glavin, not in a playground in Cambridge, Mass., but here in Dublin, in the back of a church off Molesworth Street, a church where Bram Stoker was baptized.

—How did you find this place?—

Glavin wants to know, but I ain't saying, dribble the ball beyond the foul line and sink a jumper from twenty feet.

—Make it, Tony, I say, passing him the basketball.

—Go on, he says, shooting the ball, swoosh, later hooking one off the backboard to give me an H.

O, Glavin, I think, now it is time to get a letter.

But the verger appears:

—Who are you? How did you get here? —

Lazarus

After the Son of God brought him back from
the dead, Lazarus picked up his palette
and walked off into the alleyways of
the city, dazed and unsure if he were

alive or dead, an after-thought from God
or one of the chosen who comes back to
life with an impossibly complex tale
of the dark night of the soul-surviving.

But what if that is not what he wanted,
what if Lazarus preferred to die now,
leaving the mortal coil for that other

world beyond the pale, what if he preferred
that people, including Jesus, left him
alone to die, no longer of the quick?

I Told You So

I don't want to say
That I told you so, but—

The River

Go down to the river, and wash there in it, go down to it, the river runs over you, like a wave, like a current, wave after wave, like a crest, a caress, go down there to the river, and if you are not drowned, you're saved, my brothers and sisters, you are washed clean by it, set free, you are set free, in the river and by the river, so help me, you are liberated, go down there and you'll see, the river will buoy you, hold you up, take you down, take you there, see the bottom and rise up to the top of it all, the river will guide you home, be there in its watery arms, its embrace, hold you in it, send you back along its currents, and find the shore, guide you towards your home, testify, be witness, be the light, eternal fire, be your oxygen, your net, a chest of hope, its charity, its good, taking you out, bringing you back, and then again back out, until you are whole, confident, alive, my sisters and brothers, you will become spirit yourself, imbued with the river, imbibing its water, talk to it, listen to its answers, its advice, that's the river I know, the one I walked into when I was ready to, asking for help and love, the river was there for me, as it was there for you, your guide, your star, that's the river, that's it, my brothers and sisters, my sisters and brothers, that is it, the river right there, waiting for you.

Morning Light Through Saloon Windows

I was there to drink, I was never there
For the conversation, much as I made
Believe that I was there for the good talk,
I was there to get hammered, seek my end
In oblivion and beyond, to do
It again the next day, and the next one
After that until I died, which even
If premature, I figured that it was worth
Every miserable second, but
 It was not worth it, it was not worth it,
Not worth a thing, if anything, it was
Worthless, an illusion, as most of life
Was, after all I was not there to chat
With the neighbors, I was just there to die.

What I Miss

I miss seeing the kestrel around me
Up overhead, as quick as a blink or
A glance across the heath in the blue sky
Of an English afternoon in London
North of Gospel Oak, walking with others
Out to take the air before the rain comes,
I miss strawberries, inexpensive herbs,
Sicilian lemons, French apples, parsley
From Peter Stephens (no relation, though
I have an older brother by that name),
I miss Portuguese sardines in olive
Oil, Duchy organic hamburgers, spring
Greens, Bendick's chocolates, and I miss you
When I'm back in London, and you are here.

The Scarlet Tanager

I return from tooling around the park
and doing miscellaneous errands
(really this is an errant ride without

destination to speak of), though I may
have a weak cappuccino with a friend
before heading back home from Riverside

Park, anything to avoid sitting down
and writing once again, and again blank
pages, blank verses, blank walls and blank doors

without door knobs, not to mention door-frames
without doors, so that to speak of this day
as miscellaneous is to miscount

the blessings, mistaken facts for a bird.
Was it really a scarlet tanager?

Six Million

There are six million monarch butterflies
in that meadow, six million beats heartwise
every ten days or so, six million
ways to love you, and I am not kidding,

around the night, there are six million stars
to be counted before morning, this field
covered by six million yellow flowers,
daffodils, nasturtiums, tulips, and more,

six million ways to score a touchdown or
to score a basket, six million faces
in this city, six million recipes
for making bread, or six million other

ways of not saying there were six million
of them, but there were six million to die,
be killed, vanish, disappear from the world,
there really were six million...six million...

Herons Amid Gladiolas

In a certain light at a particular
hour around this time of year, and
in this part of the world, gladiolas
blossom, and then the herons come.

Sometimes people will say that the herons
look like flowers, while others might observe
its opposite, noting how heronlike the gladiolas.

What is most striking is to see herons
amid the gladiolas, the long necks
of the birds, the long stems of the flowers,
mimicking each other. That makes living

here almost like it was a dream, and when
you dream, it is about living right here
among the gladiola and heron.

Lunch

Friday:
Fried egg

The Tao Of The Taoiseach

Lie like a bandit,
laugh at the facts,
leave Galway
and don't come back.

Enda's off to Dublin,
he left Castlebar
far behind,
he likes to make jokes

nowadays about Lumumba,
whose heirs live in Tallaght,
that's the kind of guy
he's become, the kind of

man he is, it's the tao
of this taoiseach,
where the rich overreach,
and the poor bitch

and moan, knocking a tin
cup against the spikes
on a metal fence,
to keep the likes of us

away from the likes of them,
ladylike hems on their dresses,
manlike grunts as they guzzle
pints, griping about workers,

moaning about the lower and
middle classes, while attending
art classes themselves, so cultured,
they are, and yet so artless.

There Is No Muse Like This Muse

I have been sending mixed messages to
The Muse, which is my fault entirely, so
Please forgive me for seeming this way, O
Sweet Muse, about whom there has never been
Any other, of that I am certainly
Sure, there is no Muse like this Muse, no Muse
At all if it is not this very one,
The Muse to whom I dedicate these words.

And so I go out and walk among the
People, *my people*, with noses and eyes
And mouths just like my nose and eyes and mouth,
Though none of them has big feet or streaming
Ginger-colored hair, none are able to
Stand in for the Muse if she gets the flu.

Sailing To Brooklyn

When I saw my Irish aunt, a widow,
And no longer working, I realized that
Einstein was right—not only space, but time
Was relative, and I saw how it had

Raced ahead with the old aunt in one sense,
And then completely slowed down in other
Ways: she was as old as the hills in voice,
Face, clothing, and other respects, yet as

We sat in her Brooklyn parlor sipping
Tea and eating stale butter cookies (she
Called them biscuits), if you looked around her

Flat, it was as if time itself had stopped
Ticking forward around 1905,
When she sailed alone to America.

The Migration Of Birds

I am in love with the day because of
The clear light or the blue sky and your eyes
Or I am in love with the white clouds and
The muted colors of the leaves on the
Trees and the migration of birds in air
And on the ground and in the trees and dogs
Barking or dogs running about or just there or
This park bench off to the side away from
Everyone this pond full of ducks and coots
The imperious swans and the humble
Geese and even the majestic herons
And I love the smell in the air and chill
Behind the sunlight and I love this bench
As you sit there talking about these things

Finn McCoole

Firm Finn
fantailing
fishtailing
on the skids

McCoole's
mackerel grin
grim mornings
awake arise

attend to kine
for kin and kith
Attack the kerns
who unkindly raid

Be brave
even amid fear
Be stout
no doubt be strong

Where is she shivering
in linens maiden
made his by force
of conquest's drifts?

There in the field
she lay among sheep
sleeping her share
of breath-fogged air

Danny Boy

Londonderry air:
London derriere

Pre-Owned

It was, as it were,
As is, as if, i.e.,

Take it or leave it

What Is Light

What is light next to your light or what is
Day next to you or what is it about
The day that unfolds like a Chinese screen
And blue skies there is a breeze to the day

Alive with dogs and people and other
Things like poetry maybe even love
And these things are not so much talked about
As they imbue all the green things around

This world as the day unfolds and winds
Down the light fades as a coolness settles
Across the landscape children's voices in

The air birds singing in the trees dogs bark
A trace of coolness settling down on us
And the light the light what is light is you

After A Merce Cunningham Concert In London

Maybe we do these things out of a thought
To another world where we were made whole,

Not isolated from ourselves or from
Each other, so perhaps all art is that

Other self looking to become once more
Joined up to our dreams or our memories.

All art is autobiography—
All words, all poems, all stories, paintings,

Sculpture, music—everything is art
Potentially, even isolated

Tropes of dance, separated from the world,
Their mother ship, searching for home, even

That is autobiographically
Calling out for links to another self.

Pearly Luster

The birds are in the trees, calling and re-
Calling, whistling and singing all about,
Alive and indifferent to our pain
And suffering, which to them is no doubt

An option, though only distantly so,
While we worry ourselves out of the world
And all it is worth, we even worry
About worry itself, worrying of

Nothing more than the thought of this worry,
As the birds fly up to the blue of sky
And the pearly luster of the day's clouds,

Flying back again to a tree outside
Her window where she sits in a lightless
Room writing these thoughts into a notebook.

The Jumpshooter's Nightmare

Middle of the night in the middle of
A dream, in the middle of the basket-
Ball court, down by two with three seconds left,

Give me the ball, you shout to the forward,
Give me the fucking ball, man, I'm going
For three from downtown, stutter step, it's in.

But instead of a swish from forty feet,
Steph Curry wakes in a cold sweat, angel
Of misery whispering in his ear:

Le Bron, Le Bron, Le Bron James, Le Bron James…

Susan's Sonnet

You took the Tube to Heathrow that morning,
and it was raining when I said goodbye
at the Belsize station on Haverstock
Hill, and it has rained ever since you left
to visit family in Chicago.

The sun has not come out for days on end,
and the neighborhood is sodden and grey,
my nights are spent missing you, wishing you
were back here, home, for that is what London
is to us finally—our place, a home.

We need shampoo, vitamins, health store food,
like Red Mill eight-grain cereal, Lever
2000 soap, and Smart Wool socks, nothing
else really, just you and the sun shining.

A Bad Case Of The Blues

Loneliness kills more people than cancer,
More souls leave their bodies from it than war,
And yet the only way it is addressed
Is in syrupy country songs, jukebox
Suicide, put in a coin, push button,
You are sat alone in the corner of
The bar's long hall and feel sorry for your
Poor self, misery's cousin, mother
Of anxiety and father to none
But the dispossessed, the outcast, alone
And forgotten, alone and, well, alone.
Is there a country music song for this?
At the knife-edge of existence, who is
It out there to lend this poor soul a hand?

What Is Possible

There is a now famous poem in which
The writer seems to revel in the sensual
Moment of the natural world around
Him, only to end the poem saying

That he has wasted his life. How is that
Possible, I want to ask, if not to
The nearest person to me, then myself
I want to ask, how is that possible?

But who am I to ask, I've been a tramp
Nearly all of my life, from childhood up
To the present, now an intellectual

Tramp slouching towards the almost endgame,
And though I still believe that my life was
Not all wasted, how is that possible?

The Lark

The new light streams through the life-affirming
Windows, a blue tit in the bare branches
Of the liburnum, a noisy lorry

Outside, even before light penetrates
The morning, while out there a winter lark
Sings, two magpies eye it suspiciously,

And while the day threatens rain, the light does
Not comprehend what these other plans of
Nature are. For the lark, life is just that:

A lark. But for me, the lark is itself
Life, and nothing else, and what I see out
Winter windows is what I comprehend.

Magpies chase the bird away, the light comes
On, the day moves forward, I go about.

Just Now But Not Always

If we keep loving them, will they still keep
Bombing and shooting us, and the answer
Is simple enough, yes, they will keep up
The shooting and bombing, even chopping

Off our heads and stabbing the old people
And the youngest among us, and they will
Say it is because we bomb and shoot them,
Which is true, as we do bomb and shoot them.

But to say that there is no solution
Is not true or to say it has always
Been like this and always will be like this

Is equally not true, it has not been
Like this forever and it will not be
Just this way always and forever more.

A Pig On The Sofa

Most of my adult life I have quoted—
Or really misquoted—a Flannery
O'Connor line, saying that something was

Obvious as a pig on a sofa,
When what she wrote was quite differently
Stated, namely that it was as "plain as

A pig on a sofa," though you might think
A pig is a pig, plain or obvious,
It shouldn't be sitting on the sofa.

Gravity

The ghost may have been an angel, he thought,
Or maybe a mouse easing its way out
Of here into a more lucrative spot,
Somewhere where crumbs are morsels or even

Big pieces of cake left on the living
Room rug. The angel may be the lady
Who used to live there. But he is not there,
He is here, far away, across the sea,

And it is winter and the waves are rough,
The wind bites meanly at us all, old and
Young, even the rich grow weary and cold

Pushing up against it, one more real force
That's as invisible as her angel
Or ghost, its gravity pulling us down.

The Empty Room

She is not there anymore, and he is,
But he is not all there, hearing her there
When she is not, thinking her there, but she

Is gone, though he smells her scent in the air,
Tastes her amid the nothingness of rooms
Empty of her aura, and he even

Sees her, but it is only illusion,
For she has left, never to return here,
So that the empty rooms are chilly with

Her absence, even as his mind fills up
With that same absence of who she once was.

Shooting Star In The Blue Night's Sky

The spirit is not so much within us
As it is bursting to get out, and so

We meet people whose aura cascades all
Around them, almost like a rainbow or

Sunburst after spring rains. They cannot be
Held captive by the body, but need to

Go outwards from it, leaving their tired
Flesh almost the way a stripper leaves a

Dress pooled in the stage light, bursting her skin,
Its particulars, like dreaming awake,

Like a shooting star in the blue night's sky.

Your Mouth Is A Wave

You are the lake and its paths along which
I stroll, your thighs like the trees by the shore,
Your eyes are like two sparrows in that tree,

A linden, and your mouth is a wave which
Breaks on the shore, the mounds of sand like breasts,
The plug down which water gurgles and then

Disappears is your belly button, light
In the sky, tendrils that envelop you,
Your skin is the bark of a rare kind of

Tree whose name I can find in no sort of
Book, and your hands and feet are like flowers
Growing out of the sandy ground at shore

Line, your long arms and legs like the white clouds
That pass by on this ordinary day.

Urbane

At the end of the night, just before day
Breaks open again, the sound of alarms
Going off, where only the day before,

The sound of multiple cardinals sang,
Taking the night away from the darkness
And giving it to the first glimpses of

The new day which was about to begin.

The Muse As Castalian Spring

Full cup from the Castalian spring, what
Golden Apollo plied him with, the cup
Of the Muse, and O blue-foot, what cup of
Apollo do you drink, espresso or
Cappuccino, and does the caffeine fuel
Your nerves as tightly as a bow, fiddle,
Or guitar, if I pluck you, what pluck
Do I try to make you sing this new song
Of love, life, and poetry, every
Thing in between that goes down into the
Short weeds and the curly stalks of delta
Songs and these other alluvial songs
And springs, Castalian and otherwise,
And is this autumn the spring of the Muse?

M. G. STEPHENS is the author of twenty books, including the critically acclaimed novel *The Brooklyn Book of the Dead*; the memoir *Lost in Seoul*; and the award-winning essay collection *Green Dreams*. His play *Our Father* ran on Theatre Row (42nd Street) for over five years, and has been produced several times in Chicago, Los Angeles, and London. He was born in Washington, D.C. and grew up in Brooklyn and further out on Long Island. He has degrees from the City College of New York, Yale University, and the University of Essex in Colchester, England. Stephens taught in many writing programs, including Columbia, New York, and Princeton universities, as well as the University of London. He has also worked in the U.S. Merchant Marines, as a gas-pump jockey, a boxing writer, a greens' keeper, carpenter's apprentice, Manhattan air conditioning installer, dishwasher, short-order chef, bartender, bouncer, Lower East Side Christmas-tree salesman, night watchman, runner, typist, editor, proofreader, translator, bodyguard, dog-sitter, painting-watcher, gallerist, collagist, and provocateur.

www.ingramcontent.com/pod-product-compliance
Lightning Source LLC
Chambersburg PA
CBHW020943090426
42736CB00010B/1237